KAYAKING *in Paradise*

JOURNEYS FROM ALASKA
THROUGH THE INSIDE PASSAGE

KAYAKING in Paradise

JOURNEYS FROM ALASKA through the INSIDE PASSAGE

Text by Greg Rasmussen

Photographs by Grant Thompson, Neil Gregory-Eaves

and Peter McGee

WHITECAP BOOKS

Vancouver/Toronto

Edited by Elaine Jones
Proofread by Elizabeth McLean
Cover and interior design by Carbon Media
Maps by Alex Duffield
Printed and bound in Canada

Canadian Cataloguing in Publication Data
Rasmussen, Greg
    Kayaking in paradise

    Includes index
    ISBN 1-55110-633-7

    1. Rasmussen, Greg – Journeys – British Columbia – Pacific
Coast. 2. Kayaking – British Columbia – Pacific Coast. 3.
Kayaking – Alaska. 4. Kayaking – Washington (State) I. Title
GV776.15.B7R37 1997   797.1'224'091643   C97-910655-9

We acknowledge the support of the Canada Council for the Arts for
our publishing program and the Cultural Services Branch of the
Government of British Columbia in making this publication possible.

This book is dedicated to the people we met along the way.

Contents

Introduction

Most of us have a dream tucked away in our minds — from owning a modest cabin in the woods to being able to launch a full-scale assault on Mount Everest. For the people involved in this book, the ongoing dream is the exploration of the spectacular stretch of coast from Alaska to Washington State.

Many of the places photographed and described in these pages were visited on a three-month-long expedition that began in Alaska and ended in Vancouver, B.C. A number of people took part in that three-month journey, but photographers Neil Gregory-Eaves and Peter McGee covered it from start to finish.

That expedition was partly an exploration and mapping trip for the B.C. Marine Trail Association. The association is working toward establishing a network of sites along the British Columbia coast geared to kayaks and other small craft. Many places along the coast have already been designated for other uses — from private property to fish farms — and the Marine Trail Association wants to ensure people will continue to have access to our incredible coastline in perpetuity.

Every kayak trip doesn't have to be a major expedition, and we also explore some of the more accessible spots on the coast. It's surprising how easy it is to find solitude close to major urban centers. A sunset paddle in Vancouver's English Bay or a weekend trip to the San Juan Islands are also adventures in their own right. Over the last few years we have taken a number of trips — long and short — to the Queen Charlotte Islands, the west coast of Vancouver Island and the Gulf and San Juan islands. Photographer Grant Thompson took many of the photos in the Queen Charlotte Islands and West Coast of Vancouver Island sections of the book. Grant has spent many years paddling the coast, and is the owner/operator of Tofino Expeditions, a kayak touring company.

There is tremendous value in getting out on the water and falling into the rhythm of paddling along an isolated stretch of shoreline. Testing your physical limits, setting your day according to the ebb and flow of the tides, falling asleep in your tent to the sound of waves breaking on a nearby shoreline all serve to restore some of what is lost in daily urban life. Be warned though, once you get a taste of this patch of paradise, it can easily become an addiction.

Alaska

LeConte Bay and Frederick Sound

Clear blue skies and brilliant sunshine make for a bright day on
the water, but it's still chilly at LeConte Bay as the icy surroundings
couple with near-freezing water temperatures.

The smell of ice was in the air as we dipped our paddles into the frigid waters off Mitkof Island near Petersburg, Alaska. After months of planning and preparation, our boats were finally in the water, heading up a narrow inlet toward LeConte Bay and the southernmost calving glacier on the Pacific coast. It was July and the inlet was choked with ice, creating a surreal setting as we steered our boats past giant free-floating ice-islands, many of which easily dwarfed our six-metre-long (20-foot) sea kayaks. The steep walls of the inlet were scarred by striations made at a time when the glacier had extended farther down the channel. Somewhere up ahead of us sat the glacier itself, a distant thunder, shedding huge chunks of ice into the ocean.

Mitkof Island lies near the 57th parallel in southeast Alaska, about 190 kilometres (120 miles) south of Juneau. Our starting point was Petersburg, a town of about 3,300 which relies mainly on fishing for its livelihood. Tourism

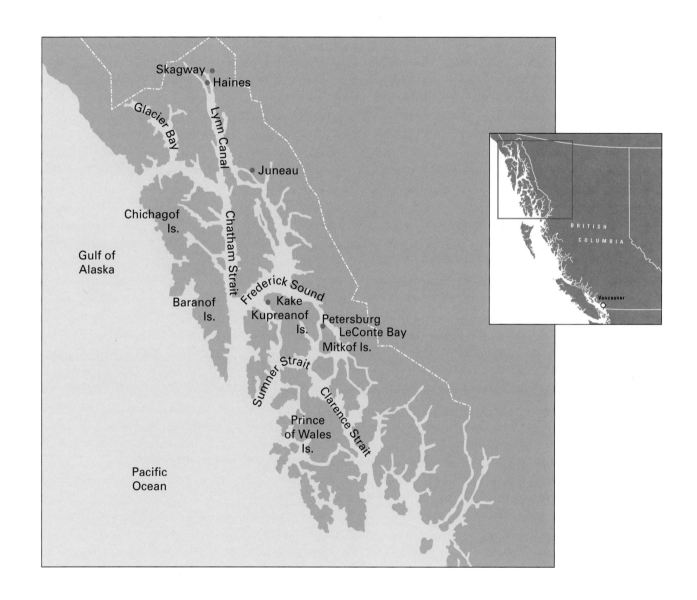

Skagway

Haines

Glacier Bay

Lynn Canal

Juneau

Chichagof
Is.

Chatham Strait

Gulf of
Alaska

Frederick Sound

Baranof
Is.

Kake

Kupreanof
Is.

Petersburg

LeConte Bay

Mitkof Is.

Sumner Strait

Clarence Strait

Prince
of Wales
Is.

Pacific
Ocean

BRITISH
COLUMBIA

Vancouver

Above: Deck space is at a premium as northbound travelers set up their tents and camp out on deck to save the cost of a stateroom.

Left: Alaska Marine Highway Ferries make regular trips up the coast from Washington State, with a stop in the Canadian Port of Prince Rupert.

is also growing in the area, but most sightseers don't venture far from the ships that bring the bulk of them to the town. Mitkof Island and its larger neighbor to the north, Kupreanof Island, offered up a collection of welcoming bays and inlets for us to explore.

Thousands of years ago, rain and snow that had fallen in the mountains near Frederick Sound had been trapped in LeConte Glacier. Now, after many years spent creeping toward the sea, centuries-old water was finally being released into the salty Pacific

Traveling by Sea Kayak

Sea kayaks are a great way to see the coastline because they can get in close to shore, glide over shallow areas and sneak into those tight spots around icebergs. Northern waters were the birthplace of kayaks — developed out of necessity in a land where there were no trees to carve canoes from. Driftwood was collected and formed into a frame that was covered with sealskins. Each boat was unique and crafted for the needs of the person using it and the waters where it would be paddled. Kayaks feel a bit unstable to the uninitiated, but with practice they are safe even in fierce seas. Traditionally, seals, fish and even whales were hunted from kayaks by northern people from the Aleutian Islands to Greenland. There is even evidence to suggest early paddlers ventured far to the south in these amazing boats.

Top-heavy icebergs are another hazard of paddling near calving glaciers. Melting can shift the balance, causing the massive bergs to roll over unexpectedly.

Clear and ice cold, spring runoff cascades down a ravine into Frederick Sound.

Ocean. All around us there were collisions of ice, air and water. It melted and dripped into the oceans from overhangs, and fractured with cracking sounds. Occasionally, a hiss of air would emerge from a hidden pocket warmed by the sun.

As we paddled, the icy water dripped down our paddles and onto the spray skirts of our boats. Smaller pieces of ice all around us struck the fiberglass hulls of our kayaks with a sharp tapping sound. There was no danger of a *Titanic*-style collision, but there was a hazard in another form. Many of the icebergs were precariously top-heavy, and a number of times we saw them unexpectedly topple over with a massive splash. It was spectacular, but something we wanted to avoid witnessing at close range.

This was just our first day on the water, but already the trip was surprising us, paying off even greater dividends than we had hoped for as we planned the expedition over the preceding winter. Only a week earlier we had been caught up in a frenzy of last-minute activity: making sure the boats were properly equipped, camera gear was working, and all the details of our lives were wrapped up. This was the start of a major trip that would take three months to complete and cover hundreds of kilometres of coastline. It was now July and we wouldn't arrive at our final destination of Vancouver, B.C. until early October. One recent bleary-eyed evening had been spent covering everything in the kitchen (including us) with

Fireweed grows abundantly at Wrangell Narrows. Coastal natives ate the central pith of this plant in early spring. Mature fireweed was harvested for the fibers in its outer stem, which were soaked and then spun into twine. The seed fluff was mixed with dog hair and woven into blankets or clothing.

pancake mix as we measured and scooped three months' worth of breakfasts into individual plastic bags. Aside from the mess in the kitchen, our lungs felt as if they were coated in dough after sucking excess air out of the baggies to save precious cargo space.

But now as we sat with our fully packed boats low in the water, all the details and anxiety faded away. The ice and steep cliff walls served to protect us, providing us with calm seas in which to contemplate our spectacular surroundings. There was so much ice that getting close to the face of the glacier proved impossible as one channel after another led nowhere. We paddled as close to the glacier as we could until finally our boats were penned in. The clock was ticking, and soon we had to head back to camp before we were trapped in the ice by shifting winds and an incoming tide.

It was a morning none of us will soon forget, and it left us in high spirits. Paddling through the ice that day brought back the words of naturalist John Muir, a glacier aficionado and explorer. In 1879, Muir had visited Alaska's Glacier Bay and marveled at its beauty and its effect on him:

"The green waters of the fiord were filled with sun-spangles; the fleet of icebergs set forth on their voyages with the upspringing breeze; and on the innumerable mirrors and prisms of these bergs, and on those of the shattered crystal walls of the glaciers, common white light and rainbow light began to burn, while the mountains shone in their frosty jewelry, and loomed again in

Glaciers and glaciation

Up until 10,000 years ago, glaciers such as this one at LeConte Bay covered almost all of Canada and Europe and were radically reshaping the landscape. They scoured away soil and carved up rocks in one place and deposited them in another. There are many telltale marks of glaciers up and down the coastline, but the most notable are the striations, or scars, they made in rock faces as they advanced down the coast.

Glaciers are far from static slabs of ice — they ebb and flow over the decades. A striking example of this is Glacier Bay, Alaska, which was a wall of ice when first seen by European explorers in 1794. But when the area was next surveyed in 1877 the glacier had retreated a full 70 kilometres (44 miles), exposing the bay for the first time in eons. John Muir, who explored the area in 1879–80, was astounded by the newly born landscape, where trees had yet to sprout on the hills and where the beaches were so new they weren't yet littered with driftwood. Since then the ice has retreated another 60 kilometres (38 miles) into the mountains, leaving Glacier Bay exposed until the next climate shift and the return of the ice.

Striations made by a glacier in the rock cliffs above LeConte Bay show how far this massive glacier once extended.

Far from the actual face of the calving glacier, ice spills out of LeConte Bay, near Petersburg. The bay is the home of the southernmost calving glacier on the Pacific coast.

the thin azure in serene terrestrial majesty. We turned and sailed away, joining the outgoing bergs...and our burning hearts were ready for any fate, feeling that, whatever the future might have in store, the treasures we had gained this glorious morning would enrich our lives forever."

The writing might be a bit flowery for these times, but John Muir had been trying the impossible — to take others to his Alaska, to convey the feeling you can only get from being in a particular place at a particular time, and losing yourself wholly in your surroundings. Here we were a hundred years later, and suddenly even his "overwritten" prose failed to come close to adequately describing the majesty of our surroundings. His closing words would prove to be the unofficial motto for the rest of the trip, often coming to mind when things turned ugly for one reason or another. No matter what might happen, the treasures we had already gained would be reward enough.

After a few days paddling and camping near LeConte Glacier, we headed up Frederick Sound, around the tip of Kupreanof Island, and on to the small town of Kake, where we witnessed another spectacular show, this time in the form of salmon pooling at the mouth of a creek running through the town.

It was raining as we made our way toward the creek mouth, and occasionally the steady patter of raindrops on water was interrupted by the splash of a

pink salmon leaping from the depths. As we drew closer to shore, the number of skybound salmon increased until it appeared to be raining fish all around us, enveloping us in a sound akin to thousands of buckets of water being dumped onto the ocean's surface. Everywhere we looked, salmon were breaking the surface. Near shore we noticed we could feel them through the hulls of the kayaks, swimming just beneath the surface, being pushed upwards by those below. It was astonishing to think we were literally riding on the backs of thousands upon thousands of salmon, inwardly compelled to return to their birthplace after years at sea.

Up ahead, on the shore, lumbering black shapes came into view in the fading light. The best-fed black bears in the world were lounging by the side of the river, their bellies drooping with the weight of fish. They would walk in, select a salmon for the kill and take it to a convenient rock where they would eat only the richest part, the belly, leaving the rest for the gulls. It was an exhilarating example of bounty and decadence, and it left us speechless. We sat in our boats, soaked with rain and the splash of fish echoing in our ears, watching the bears feed until darkness fell and it was time to paddle back to camp.

Fish, ice and bears are some of the things you might expect to find in Alaska, and we found them all in a short time. We could have happily spent the summer paddling Alaskan waters, but time was short and we had many crossings to make and islands to explore to the south. We returned to Petersburg, and made our way south for the next leg of the trip.

Left: Salmon returning to spawn are plucked from the waters and processed in a frenzy of activity. Much of the roe in these buckets will end up in Asian markets.

Above: It's much easier fishing from a double kayak than a single. Here, one person battles a ling cod, while the other controls the boat.

Ice

Many a northern town owes its origins to the quest for gold or other precious minerals, but at least one Alaska town traces its beginnings to a good supply of ice. Norwegian Peter Bushmann knew a good block of ice when he saw one, and he liked the quality of ice he saw when he happened upon LeConte Glacier. In the days before refrigeration, he realized boats could be packed with the clean, clear ice to keep salmon fresh while they were out at sea. To take further advantage of this natural resource he built a cannery. Other Norwegians soon followed in Bushmann's tracks, bringing their families and establishing Petersburg as a fishing center. Although plenty of fish are still processed in the town, the ice from the glacier is no longer used commercially.

The commercial wharves at Petersburg come to life in the summer as the salmon and tourists speed up the pace of commerce on the Alaskan coast.

The North and Mid Coast

Prince Rupert to Cape Caution

A humpback whale puts on a show before heading to the bottom
to feed in Laredo Channel. Up to 16 metres (53 feet) in length,
these giants range from southern Mexico to the Chukchi Sea in
the north. They sometimes feed by "bubble netting" — releasing
air bubbles while swimming in a circle below their prey of krill
or small schooling fish. The bubbles help concentrate the feed
before the whales swim through for their meal.

We were paddling toward what has to be one of British Columbia's smallest towns — Oona River — about 25 kilometres (16 miles) southwest of Prince Rupert on Porcher Island. It had been a long day on the water and our bodies were aching from paddling against a head wind for hours on end. As we entered the river mouth and headed toward the government dock, we were rewarded with a strangely beautiful sunset tinting the sky in wild shades of purple accented by wispy clouds.

We weren't sure what kind of reception we would get in this remote community, which is distinguished by a massive logging clear-cut on the slopes behind the town, and the first person we saw on the dock made us think twice about sticking around. He was a fierce-looking character, the kind of guy you expect to see with a chain saw in one hand and a bloodied fishing gaff in the other. The dock shook as his massive frame made a bee-line toward us and our boats.

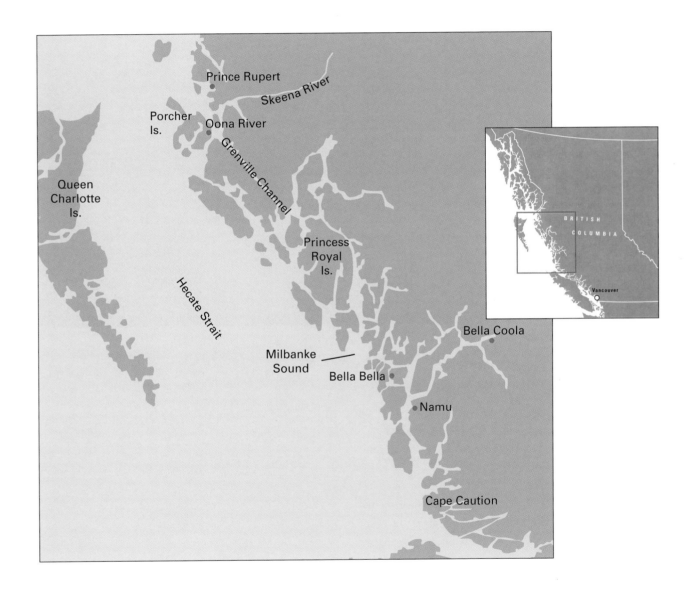

Prince Rupert

Skeena River

Porcher
Is.

Oona River

Grenville Channel

Queen
Charlotte
Is.

Princess
Royal
Is.

Hecate Strait

Bella Coola

Milbanke
Sound

Bella Bella

Namu

Cape Caution

BRITISH
COLUMBIA

Vancouver

"So, like, where are you all headed?" said an unexpectedly friendly voice coming from somewhere inside his bearded face.

"Umm, er, we're actually heading down the coast — to Vancouver," one of us replied, breaking out of a stupor.

"Cool," he said. "Well, if you need a place to pitch your tents I've got lots of room up at my place."

And so we met Ralph, the unofficial welcoming committee for Oona River, population 35. That was just the beginning of the town's hospitality. Within minutes of arriving we had a campsite, the offer of a soak in a hot tub and an invitation to breakfast. It was just one of the many examples of overwhelming warmth we encountered as we traveled the coast. Our first impression of Ralph was a reminder of the dangers of attaching labels to people too quickly. Kayaker, logger, fisherman — each with preconceived notions that go

Above: We weren't having any luck with our rods and reels in Petrel Channel, but this friendly fisherman saved the day by giving us four salmon.

Right: This shallow bay looks almost tropical — an illusion that's dispelled when you jump in. The water temperature doesn't vary much from 10° Celsius (50° Fahrenheit) throughout the year.

Bull Kelp

There used to be a lot more kelp beds like this one along the west coast, but like other natural resources, they have been greatly reduced by human interference. Surprisingly, the sea otter trade, which began in the late 18th century, has a great deal to do with the decline of kelp beds. One of the primary food sources of sea otters is the spiny, bottom-dwelling sea urchin. When the otters were hunted out of existence along most of the coast, sea urchin populations surged exponentially. Sea urchins feed on the bottom of the kelp where it anchors to underwater rocks, so it wasn't long before kelp beds, lush with marine plants and animals, were turned into underwater barrens.

Bull kelp beds fill a number of important roles — some obvious and many subtle. Anchored up to 45 metres (150 feet) below the surface, kelp beds are referred to as "forests" — and you only have to dive among these towering plants to see why. They protect young fish from larger predators, provide a place for fish to lay their eggs, and help to calm the ocean surface by regulating the waves as they break and rebound from shore. Almost all rockfish depend on kelp in some way.

Kelp and other "seaweeds" are actually different forms of many-celled marine algae. Bull kelp is a brown algae; red algae seaweeds live in even deeper waters and green algae plants live in more shallow waters. Bull kelp can grow at the incredible rate of half a metre (20 inches) per day in good conditions and reach lengths of 50 metres (165 feet) or more.

The bulbous sac floating on the surface is called a pneumatocyst and contains the same types of gases found in the atmosphere: oxygen, nitrogen and carbon dioxide. It keeps the energy-producing blades near the surface so photosynthesis can take place, producing energy that travels down the stipe (stem) to the parts of the plant too deep for sunlight to reach.

along with it. Kayakers are a bunch of weekend environmentalists. Loggers are short-sighted pillagers of the environment. And fishermen will take the last fish in the ocean for a dollar. Spending time in a place like Oona River permits reality to set in, loosening the glue on some of those labels.

Just as the people can seem a bit rough around the edges at first, the landscape on the north coast seems harsh on the surface as well. It's battered by fierce winds, drenched with seemingly endless rains, and can be very unforgiving if you make a mistake. But on a calm summer's day it can seem the most gentle environ imaginable. We spent a number of weeks here, working our way steadily south, hopping between islands and following the coast. Many days were trials of endurance, fighting wind, rain and tricky seas. But on some days the swells would even out, the wind would die and we could tuck in near the rocky shoreline. Paddling alongside a massive bed of kelp, reveling in the isolation, we were aware of how priceless this raw and remote wilderness is.

There's no doubt the environment has shaped the character of those who settle here. They're pragmatic for the most part, hard working and not afraid to speak their minds. In an overpopulated world, the north coast of B.C. is an anomaly. Fewer people live here today than 50 years ago. That's because many of the jobs that were once here have disappeared, especially those in the fishing and logging industries. In the early 20th century there were several dozen fish canneries along the coast. Every summer, hundreds of workers would make the trip up the coast to work in the canneries as the salmon made their way to rivers such as the Skeena to spawn. But freezer boats and large plants in the south eliminated the need for on-location canning, and the plants were closed one by one.

At about the same time, the small family-run logging outfits, the hand loggers, began to be replaced by big companies that controlled large chunks of land and were based somewhere else. Hopes of new settlements, vibrant young communities in the wilderness, fell by the wayside with a whimper rather than a bang. People stopped coming and the plants were stripped of equipment and left to rot away. Those who have stayed in places such as Namu and Oona River are not there chasing the pot of gold, but rather pursuing a different lifestyle than what is found "down south" or "outside."

You can see change in the works on this section of coast, though. Paddling into Shearwater Marina near Bella Bella, we found a newly built hotel and brand-new docks to cater to the pleasure boaters plying the coast. A bit farther south we were welcomed into St. John's Fishing Lodge, where we had a first-hand look at the new natural resource — tourists. They bring in the money to support the fishing guides, camp cooks and float-plane pilots who in a different era would have made a living as loggers or commercial fishers.

Despite this influx of tourists, there is still plenty of room to roam in northern waters. There's nothing quite like crawling out of your sleeping bag on a sunny morning and finding yourself in a place such as Kitson Island Marine Park near the mouth of the Skeena River. We sat on the beach in front of a small driftwood fire, drinking coffee and staring out at the ocean, knowing that once we left, our footprints would be erased by the incoming tide and the beach would show no signs of our presence.

That's not to say there are endless tracts of beaches with luxurious camping on the north coast. In fact, one of the hazards of paddling in this region is the lack of safe landing and camping sites. Much of the shoreline is steep and rocky,

A blanket of low cumulous clouds hangs over two paddlers near Calvert Island on the north coast.

A paddler explores the estuary at Koeye River. The small cluster of buildings was once the living quarters and offices for people mining limestone at a nearby quarry. Today the estuary provides vital habitat for a number of species, including grizzly bears.

with trees growing right down to the tide line. Once out on the water, you sometimes have to paddle for hours before reaching a beach where you can safely land a boat or set up a tent. This makes good planning in this area essential. You have to pay attention to what weather is coming and know the spots to duck into if an unexpected squall picks up.

Even with careful planning, it's hard to predict what the fickle north coast weather will do on any given day. We broke camp early one morning to get a jump on a worrisome passage across and down Milbanke Sound. The area is relatively open to the Pacific and we soon found ourselves battling three-metre (ten-foot) swells and 30-kilometre-an-hour (20 mile-per-hour) winds halfway across. To add to the danger, we had to be wary of cruise ships and other vessels that have a hard time spotting us in our low kayaks. Finally, we made it to shelter, wet and tired after a long day's paddling, with aching muscles the only casualty of the day.

Farther south, we grew anxious as we approached the legendary landmark of Cape Caution. Lying on the mainland coast, just opposite the northern tip of Vancouver Island, the area is notorious for high wind and wave action, with no place to duck for cover. Luckily, it was only a bit choppy as we made our run south, and after a foggy morning the sky cleared and we passed the cape without incident. But just south of the point that marks Cape Caution is a reminder of the fury of the place. In among the trees, high on the shore, are the rusting remains of a freighter tossed up in a fierce storm. We paddled past the wreck and landed on the edge of a large beach. As we were setting up camp for a well-earned rest, we watched as a gray whale moved into the shallows to feed, a good omen and a welcome greeting as we prepared for the final portion of our journey.

Paddlers enjoy flat calm waters on Principe Channel. Days like these are all too rare on the north coast.

Above: The coast can be a hostile environment to plant life exposed to salt spray, fluctuating temperatures and winds that often exceed 100 kilometres (60 miles) an hour. Here, some common harebells flower near a rocky outcrop alongside Higgins Passage.

Left: Wind and wave action on rocks such as these in Ogden Channel often creates strange sounds, from whistles to otherworldly slurps.

Soggy and wind-whipped

Most people who live on the west coast make jokes about the rain — after all, what else can you do about it? But when hours of rain on end turned into days of rain on end, and combined with constant exposure to salt spray, we could only wonder when the gills would sprout on our necks. Even the best rain gear can't keep you dry under these conditions. Waterproof tents get wet when you set them up in the rain, your sleeping bag picks up moisture from the tent and from you, and as for your clothes, it's soon hard to tell the so-called dry and clean ones from the old and damp ones. In the end there was little we could do but listen to the weather forecasts and hope it would get better. When the sun did come out, the beach often looked like the site of a laundromat explosion — clothing, tents, sleeping bags and soggy people strewn in the trees, over rocks and on the sand, as everyone tried to dry out before the next big downpour.

People manage to carve out a living, and an alternative lifestyle, in many remote places along the coast. Here the light fades as paddlers approach the tiny settlement of Oona River on Porcher Island. Early evening and early morning are the most likely times to find calm sea conditions.

The Three Straits

Queen Charlotte, Johnstone and Georgia

Punching through breaking surf south of Cape Caution makes
for a wet ride. Landing or launching a boat in these conditions
demands good timing and boat handling skill to stay upright.

Passing Cape Caution on our way south marked a major transition in scenery as we continued our extended paddle down the coast. We had now been on the water for more than two months. The north coast had been challenging, with its often-hostile open coast and rugged shoreline. But now we were in the waters between Vancouver Island and the mainland, and we had to prepare for a number of changes. Some of it would involve a shift in paddling conditions, but a major part of the change was psychological — going from the relative solitude of the north to more frequent encounters with civilization.

The first test was our crossing from the mainland to Vancouver Island for a supply stop at Port Hardy. We were concerned about the 40-kilometre (25-mile) crossing because we would be far from land, exposed to the weather, and in the path of a busy shipping lane. We waited a number of days for a windy spell to pass, and left early one morning in August. The

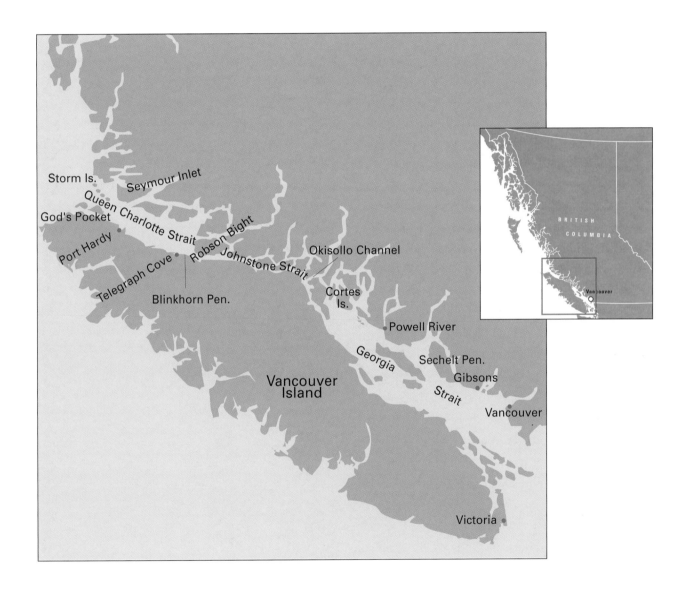

Storm Is.

Seymour Inlet

Queen Charlotte Strait

God's Pocket

Robson Bight

Port Hardy

Telegraph Cove

Johnstone Strait

Okisollo Channel

Blinkhorn Pen.

Cortes Is.

Powell River

Georgia

Sechelt Pen.

Vancouver Island

Gibsons

Strait

Vancouver

Victoria

BRITISH COLUMBIA

Vancouver

winds were light and conditions were calm when we started, but we soon found ourselves heading toward a fog bank hanging between us and our destination. We took a compass bearing off the Storm Islands, a small cluster of rocky islets in the distance, to get a reference point before we were totally enshrouded. It's not unusual to have morning fog, and usually it lifts as the day progresses, but this morning the lid was on tight and we soon lost all sight of land. We tried not to second-guess the last bearing we had taken and hoped we wouldn't be pushed off course by current, wind and tidal action and be left paddling aimlessly in the strait.

The eeriest part of the next few hours was listening as cruise ships or freighters came into hearing range with a low, steady thrumming sound. This was interspersed by the occasional blast from a ship's fog horn, which was more reassuring the farther away it was. We knew that our low-slung fiberglass boats would not show up on their radar, and it would be next to impossible for us to get out of the way if they came toward us out of the fog. We felt like bugs crawling along in the dark, knowing there's a steamroller out there somewhere, but unsure of what direction it's taking. In the end there was little we could do but paddle along, eyes glued to the deck compass, listening for any sound of the big ships.

After about four hours, some of the anxiety lifted as the Storm Islands came into view. Sea lions that

The "Inside Passage"

The passage between Vancouver Island and the mainland is often referred to as the "inside passage," but more properly, that term applies to the entire inside route up the B.C. coast to Alaska. The area between the island and the mainland is made up of three distinct areas. Queen Charlotte Strait in the north is relatively wide until it narrows dramatically, becoming Johnstone Strait. Farther south, it opens up once again and is known as the Strait of Georgia. For the sake of convenience, many people have taken to using the term "inside passage" for these three straits, so it may be necessary to clarify which "inside passage" is meant in discussing travels along the coast.

Sunset often brings with it a change in weather conditions. Wind normally blows toward shore during the day, but shifts to an offshore direction as the land cools in the evening.

Despite a large reduction in the commercial fleet, fishing remains the lifeblood of many small coastal communities. These fishermen are working the fall sockeye run in Johnstone Strait.

were hauled out on the rocks launched into the water en masse, barking loudly as we approached. At about the same time the fog began to clear and the shape of Vancouver Island materialized in the distance. Stress from being in the fog for hours, along with the physical exertion of paddling without a break, made this one of the most demanding days of the entire journey. Soon it was forgotten, though, as a dozen or so playful dolphins began leaping in the water near our boats.

After a few more hours of paddling we came into a cove called God's Pocket, one of the first anchorages south of Queen Charlotte Sound where small boats can find refuge. It doesn't offer full protection from the elements, but after the open water it's a welcome site for mariners who've been rocking and rolling in the waters to the north. We took a short break here to stretch our legs, bask in the sun and eat a well-earned late lunch before getting back into the boats and pushing on to Port Hardy for fresh supplies.

After stocking up, we spent a few days whale watching near Telegraph Cove, a historic town established during the building of a telegraph line in 1911–12. Many of the older buildings sit on stilts above the water and the wooden sidewalks are still in place. The town has been through a number of incarnations over the years. It housed work crews for the telegraph line and served as a military outpost for soldiers on the lookout for Japanese submarines during World War II. Later it was a lumber town, and more

recently it's become a base for boaters who spend the summers fishing, whale watching and cruising in nearby waters.

We set up camp about an hour's paddle away from town on the Blinkhorn Peninsula. Every day, boatloads of whale-watching tourists from Telegraph Cove would pass our campsite as they went in search of orcas. We often hopped into the kayaks and followed their lead, since the skippers were well versed on the movements of the pods. Nearby Robson Bight is famous as a location where orcas go to rub their bellies on the smooth rocks along the shallow bottom. It became a mecca for tourists in the 1980s fascinated by this unique ritual, and it was feared the huge increase in boat traffic was disrupting the whales. As a result, all boat traffic was banned in this area, leaving the whales free to scratch their itches without nosy boaters looking on.

Over the days, we were rewarded with whale sightings on a regular basis, including a couple of spectacular breaches off in the distance. One morning we were paddling along in a light swell when a pod of at least a dozen orcas overtook our boats, surfacing unexpectedly close to our kayaks. There was a momentary explosion of sound and action as their tall black fins cut the water all around us. They moved much more quickly than the gray whales we had seen farther up the coast, and within minutes they were gone.

By now we had been on the water for almost

Orcas

Unlike many other whales, orcas are aggressive predators, feeding on salmon, sea lions and even other species of whales. At times they will even thrust up onto the shore to grab a seal or sea lion, pulling it back into the water to finish the kill — one of the reasons they are also known as "killer whales." Despite this aggressive behavior, they don't pose a threat to humans.

Male orcas can easily be differentiated from the females because their dorsal fins are much larger — up to 1.5 metres (five feet) compared to one metre (three feet) for the females. They can weigh up to eight tonnes (17,500 pounds) and grow to nine metres in length (30 feet), and travel at speeds up to 48 kilometres an hour (30 miles per hour).

There are two types of orcas — resident and transient. The residents spend most of the year in a home territory and feed mostly on fish. Transients have a more varied diet and have been known to hunt cooperatively for a variety of species, including harbor seals, sea lions, whales and even sea birds.

Johnstone Strait is considered the best place in the world to view orcas because a number of pods congregate in the area to feed and socialize in the salmon-rich waters. Peak whale-watching time is April to November when residents are most common, as some of the animals move offshore during the winter months. Transients are less predictable, but can be found on the coast year-round. It's believed the transients cover a range of up to 1,500 kilometres (950 miles) along the coast.

A lot of research is being conducted into orcas' squeaky chatter of whistles and groans, which is unique to each group. Aside from humans, killer whales are the only known species with distinct dialects. Their dialects are believed to convey information about pod relationships and to maintain cohesion as they travel. Their vocalizations can be heard up to 12 kilometres (eight miles) underwater.

A bull orca surfaces near Robson Bight.

Large swells, such as this one north of Vancouver Island, give paddlers a sense of the raw energy of the open Pacific Ocean. On some days, they provide a pleasant ride, while on others they send even the largest boats scrambling for cover.

three months since we had started the journey in Alaska. The days were getting shorter and we still had a long trip ahead, so we broke camp and pressed south in the confines of Johnstone Strait. As we paddled, we encountered pods of dolphins numbering in the dozens and smaller groups of porpoises. Sometimes they rewarded us with their company, traveling alongside our boats for half an hour or more, while on other occasions they would appear and be gone again in a flash.

The narrow channels were a reminder of the power of tidal currents. As the tide rises and falls, a massive volume of water must enter and exit each channel, bay and strait. A flat calm channel can be quickly transformed by the tide into a rushing torrent full of standing waves and massive whirlpools that can literally swallow a fair-sized fishing boat. At Nakwakto Rapids near Seymour Inlet, the fastest tidal currents in the world are created as water rushes through a very narrow opening at speeds of up to 20 knots.

Timing is the key to negotiating such places, and we carefully planned our approach to another such passage, Okisollo Channel, south of Johnstone Strait. The tide here can run at 9 knots, which is far faster than we can paddle. In most places there is a period of slack tide when the water is neither rising nor falling, but here slack tide only marks a change in tidal direction. We paddled against the current, timing our arrival at the channel's choke point to coincide

Fishing

Catching a salmon in a kayak is easy — as long as you have seven hands. You need two hands on your paddle to maintain the boat's position, one for the rod, another for the reel, one to gaff the fish, one to hold it on the deck and another to give it a thwack on the head. Unfortunately most of us have only the two hands to work with, which makes fishing from a kayak anything but easy.

Just because it isn't easy doesn't mean it's not a lot of fun. Improvisation gets paddlers through many a tight spot, and fishing is no exception. Gaffs can be made by lashing pieces of driftwood together, rods can be strapped to decks with bungee cords, and elbows can be used to pin a fish down on your spray skirt. Of course, under these conditions the fish tend to win the battle a bit more often than when they're facing somebody in a bigger, more stable boat. (We won't mention the time that a certain member of our party lost rod, reel, gaff, knife and a wriggling salmon all in one fell swoop). But one thing is certain, if the battle is won, the fish tastes all the better for the effort involved.

Above: Dinner on deck. A sleek salmon drapes across the bow after a prolonged battle with a kayaking fisherman.

Left: With their boats hauled up above the high tide line and their tents set up for the night, a tour group takes a break. Tour operators often use double kayaks such as these for their increased stability and safety for novice paddlers.

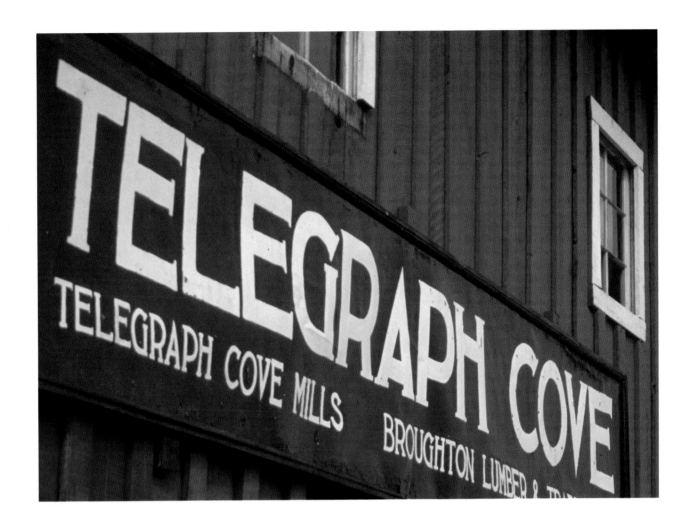

Above: Telegraph Cove has a colorful history and is a favorite with the pleasure boat crowd on Vancouver Island. Wooden boardwalks and historic buildings on stilts give the community a picturesque charm.

Left: This Princess Line cruise ship is negotiating Johnstone Strait. The passage between Vancouver Island and the mainland narrows considerably in spots, making it a tight squeeze for marine traffic.

with the tide change. As we drew closer our strongest paddle strokes were merely holding us in position. We tucked in the eddy behind a large rock and waited for the water to switch direction. In the channel we could see large whirlpools forming, swirling logs around as if they were swizzle sticks. When the tide finally changed, we popped out from behind the rock and let the current take us along at 10 knots through the upper and lower channels and into another famous section of water known as Hole in the Wall, with its narrow channel and steep rock walls. It was an adventurous eight kilometres (five miles) of water, and we were glad to have made it through without mishap.

It was now October and we had been out on the water since the beginning of July. One morning we woke to a covering of frost on our campsite. It was tough to get out of a warm sleeping bag and into a damp boat that morning, and it made us anxious to press on and put some distance behind us. But a few days of warm weather lightened the anxiety, and we relaxed at Copeland Islands Marine Park south of Cortes Island, where we witnessed a spectacular lunar eclipse as we lounged around the campfire.

The end of the major part of this trip was in sight. We stopped in at the mill town of Powell River, and then paddled hard through some of the worst seas we had encountered in months. Although they weren't as big as the large rollers up north, we were paddling through 1.5-metre (five-foot) waves, being pushed along by winds blowing 50 kilometres an hour (30 miles per hour). Many craft would have had trouble handling these conditions, but the kayaks proved their worth, taking the water well, and remaining stable with their low center of gravity as the waves broke over the top of the boats. Hours later, our wet and exhausted group reached the town of Gibsons on the Sunshine Coast. The goal was now within reach as Vancouver came into view on the horizon. Up ahead were family, friends, warm beds and food free from the annoying crunch of sand. Behind was an unforgettable collage of sights, sounds and experiences collected on our three-month journey down the coast.

Paddling into Vancouver's False Creek brought on a sense of culture shock. Our boats were dwarfed by the freighters lying at anchor and the high-rises on the shore ahead. A stream of small boats came and went from under the Granville Street Bridge. We stopped paddling for a moment to soak it all in and prepare for a return to city life. We knew other adventures were surely in store, but memories of this trip would always remain vivid. With that in mind, we dipped our paddles and headed for the beach.

How high is tonight's tide? There's nothing worse than waking up in the middle of the night with a wave knocking on the door of your tent. But dense coastal forests often mean you have to set up on the beach rather than in the protection of the trees.

Left: A moss-covered pole at Mamalilaculla on Village Island in the Broughton Archipelago.

Right: Low tide, a warm sleeping bag and a good book make for a lazy day south of Cape Caution.

There are no safe anchorages off this beach near Cape Caution, making it hostile territory for larger boats. As a result, all this un-tracked sand and beautiful flat beach is left for paddlers to enjoy.

The
Queen Charlotte
Islands

Gwaii Haanas National Park Reserve

Under a psychedelic sky, a group crosses Juan Perez Sound,
south of Lyell Island.

The Haida elder known as "Captain Gold" looked out over the calm water of the sheltered bay and told us how he felt standing amidst the disintegrating remains of the village site, a place where his ancestors had lived for thousands of years.

"The people are always at my elbow. Ever since I first paddled my canoe into this bay I have felt their presence here."

He was referring to a trip many years back when he was exploring his own roots, looking for something that was missing in his life. He had taken a canoe and set out to paddle these waters, to fish and to think, and to rediscover something. It was in this place — Ninstints — that he found it.

There are many awe-inspiring places to visit on the B.C. coast, but this former village site on one of the most remote islands in the Queen Charlotte group tends to result in more slack-jawed rapture than any other. This is due to an unparalleled combination of rich native history, remote wilderness and

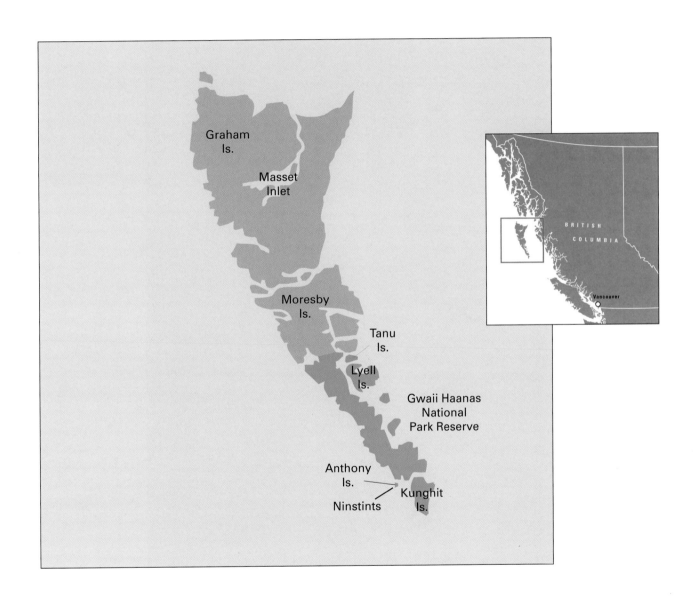

Graham
Is.

Masset
Inlet

Moresby
Is.

Tanu
Is.

Lyell
Is.

Gwaii Haanas
National
Park Reserve

Anthony
Is.

Ninstints

Kunghit
Is.

BRITISH
COLUMBIA

Vancouver

A deer looks up from feeding on the grass at the base of "Bear Mother" pole at Ninstints.

stunning scenery. It is Anthony Island on the charts, but the Haida know it as Skung Gwaii, which means "Red Cod Island."

Our journey to this small, remote island situated off the southwest corner of the Queen Charlottes started with a paddle through choppy, wind-blown seas from Rose Harbour, on Kunghit Island, where we had been dropped off by float plane. We had heard a great deal about the site and were looking forward to an afternoon wandering through the crumbling remains of the longhouses that once made up the village, and examining the fading poles.

It's a place whose very remoteness saved it from being stripped of the ceremonial poles — one of the key symbols of the Haida culture. Those poles make it the star attraction of the Queen Charlottes — a locus for daytrippers who buzz down in high-powered Zodiacs to see the poles, take a few photos and try to soak in the "Haida experience." It's easy to be cynical about people who stroll the site for a short time and claim to feel some deep connection to the place and its long-dead occupants. At the same time it's hard to spend any time here and not be moved in some way.

The village is arranged along a protected beach facing a small bay, and it's immediately obvious it is a very special place. A collection of poles, some tilting and gray with decay, stand in front of the remains of massive longhouses arranged in a line facing the beach. The majority of the poles are properly referred to as memorial or mortuary poles, and they served as burial platforms for chiefs and clan leaders. At most locations in the Charlottes, these beautifully carved poles were chopped down and carted off to museums from Switzerland to Chicago. Even here, at Ninstints, the remains inside the boxes were looted by museum collectors and treasure hunters, but at least some of the poles themselves were spared.

One of the most puzzling questions for most visitors is why the remaining poles are being allowed to decay, fall to earth and be reclaimed by the forest. They are undoubtedly priceless, and there was a fierce debate over how to protect these artifacts, the central attraction at this UNESCO World Heritage Site. But in the end, the Haida decided to allow nature to take its course, with only minimal intervention to slow the process. The Haida describe it as a "living graveyard," a place to pay respect to their ancestors, a place where nature will be allowed to prevail.

Soon after we arrived on the island we met Captain Gold, the watchman charged with protecting Ninstints and its artifacts. He invited us up to his cabin where he and his wife made coffee. We sat outside on a magnificent wooden deck, looking out over a rocky beach. He told us about his first visit to the island and his connection to the place ever since. He is a man composed of many layers — he even goes by three different names — Captain Gold; the Haida name Wanagun; and his legal name, Richard Wilson.

Captain Gold is a name with its roots planted in the early fur-trading era on the island. It was common First Nations practice to conduct a ceremony where names were exchanged in order to cement a bond with others. In this way the original Captain Gold had received the name from a trading ship's captain. The current Captain Gold had the name given to him by others familiar with the islands' history. This fits with the tradition of many north coast First Nations, where different names are used at different stages of a person's life. Like many other traditions, this was forced out of their culture by governments and missionaries who wanted to impose their own sense of order, and keep track of people from birth to death.

The newest Captain Gold's fate became intertwined with the island one day in 1973 when he first paddled his canoe into the bay, chased by a rising storm. He was on a quest of sorts, looking for a connection to his past. "I glided to a stop amongst the kelp, and right beside me, spiritually, I could feel kids diving off the rocks and swimming all around me. I could feel them watching me."

It was an overpowering experience for him, and a sign that this place would become very important in his life. He ended up working to protect Ninstints as the Council of the Haida and the Canadian government bickered over who would administer the site and how it would be protected. In 1981 the village was declared a UNESCO World Heritage Site, and an agreement was worked out between the federal government and the Haida over how conservation and tourism would be administered. Captain Gold became one of the first watchmen — Haida who watch over and protect the sacred sites in the Queen Charlottes.

There is currently a renewed interest in Haida culture in North America and elsewhere, but the history and art of the Haida have intrigued outsiders ever since Europeans made contact with them in the late 18th century. They sailed in to find a seagoing people with a strong village system, impressive artwork, a powerful mythology and a history of successful trading and war-making up and down the coast.

Archaeologists have found evidence dating occupation of the islands at least as far back as 10,000 years. Geological research shows that a land bridge between Asia and North America ran very close to the Queen Charlotte Islands some 15,000 years ago. This is likely when the first people began moving to the area and onto the North American continent itself. As the waters rose once again, the people on the islands were isolated and began developing the unique Haida culture. Over the course of time the Haida developed a high level of construction and tool-making skills along with an elaborate social structure.

Thousands of years of tradition were almost erased within a few decades after the arrival of European traders. Estimates vary, but in the 1830s tens of thousands of Haida were living on the island.

Steller's sea lions watch as kayakers pass by their haul-out south of Anthony Island. The males, at three metres (10 feet) long, can be quite intimidating when they take an interest in you. In poor weather they tend to stay in the water, but when it's calm they're often found basking on the rocks. They feed mostly on rockfish, but also eat squid, clams and salmon.

Slaves, Burial Poles and Human Sacrifice

The Haida were a slaving nation for thousands of years before contact with Europeans. Their seafaring skills allowed them to cross open water to the mainland and other islands, where they would take captives and use them as slaves in their home villages. Even today, this remains a sensitive subject among coastal native people. When a chief or other important village member died, the person's remains were ensconced in a large cedar box atop an elaborately carved cedar mortuary pole. These poles would be mounted in holes dug deep into the earth. In some cases, an unlucky slave would be forced into the pit as a human sacrifice before the pole was put in place and the hole filled with earth.

Kayakers paddle into the protected bay at Ninstints on Anthony Island, where the largest remaining group of poles in the Queen Charlottes will be left to decompose into the wilderness.

These numbers fell drastically with the introduction of new diseases. One of the earlier smallpox epidemics in the late 1830s killed one out of three Haida. Wave after wave of disease soon made ghost towns out of the once-thriving villages, killing up to 90 per cent of the people. By the 1860s smaller settlements had been abandoned entirely, and most survivors had settled in the main communities of Masset and Skidegate.

The virtual abandonment of many villages opened the door to those who coveted Haida artwork. Demand from museums around the world fueled collectors who cut the poles down in the name of preservation and carted them off to museums across the globe. Because of its remote location, however, Ninstints was spared this fate, and most of the poles remained untouched until they were officially protected.

The isolation of the southern parts of the Queen Charlottes also served to preserve the natural beauty of the place until the creation of Gwaii Haanas National Park was announced in 1987. Although difficult to reach, the south offers the best paddling in the islands. Much of the rest of the Charlottes is hostile to kayakers, especially the wild west coast where huge rollers from the open Pacific tumble in and break into sheets of white spray on the jagged, rocky cliffs.

The Charlottes have long been considered exotic and daunting for outsiders. Adventurer William Downie captured the essence of the Queen Charlottes' coastline in this description, written in 1859:

"The rocks rise like mighty giants, daring the approaching sailor to set foot on the islands they guard. They stand bold and defiant with the scars of ages seaming their sides in the shape of rifts and fissures, and, at their feet, the waters roll with a strong underswell towards the uninviting shore. But here and there a narrow inlet will admit the traveler into a small natural harbour. Also this may be surrounded by towering mountains, rearing aloft with the same threatening appearance, while here and there a waterfall, like a thundering, splashing cascade, throws its contents into the otherwise quiet harbour and makes its waters turbulent."

The beauty and fierceness that Downie describes are very much part of the lure for kayakers today. Paddling along this rugged shoreline, wary of rocks and strong currents, suddenly we would round a point and find a quiet cove in the lee of the wind. Often there was a "canoe run" leading up to the beach — an underwater path picked clean of large rocks where Haida warriors landed their massive cedar dugout canoes hundreds of years before us. Up beyond the beach, in the shelter of the big trees were plush, mossy camping spots.

It was clear that this place had been in use for a long, long time. Not weeks, or seasons, or decades, but many hundreds of years. The seagoing community of Haida men, women and children had undoubtedly ebbed and flowed here as the seasons changed. We would camp in places that used to be small villages, or summer food-gathering locations where fish were harvested and berries collected and dried. At most campsites, we found clear evidence of middens — the garbage heaps of history, where archaeologists mine for clues of the past. A variety of tools, including woodworking adzes, barbed harpoon heads and bone fishhooks dating back thousands of years, have been found at some of the locations. It's tempting for visitors to search for such prizes, but it's strictly illegal to disturb the sites.

There are also signs of more recent history. At our starting point of Rose Harbour, an old whaling station on the north of Kunghit Island, we stepped over and around the detritus of the whalers — rust-eaten iron chains, old boilers from the rendering plant, decaying wooden beams. They are reminders of what the place was for a brief period in the early 20th century. In the whaling days, when bones and carcasses littered the landscape as the blubber was rendered into oil, the smell at Rose Harbour was said to be so bad it could turn white paint to green.

Places such as Rose Harbour are visible reminders that the southern part of the Queen Charlottes is a graveyard of modern industry as well as ancient native culture. Remnants of whaling stations, canneries, logging operations and old mine sites are all melting back into the wilderness. These days Rose Harbour is a staging area for many kayakers because it is the last piece

Two paddlers scout for a landing spot in a lagoon on Gordon Island, just east of Anthony Island.

The 3-D Jigsaw Puzzle

A line of kayaks sat on the beach by the old whaling station at Rose Harbour in the southern part of the Queen Charlotte Islands. The float plane that had shuttled us down on a spectacular flight over the wild and rocky west side of the islands was going back empty to its base near Skidegate. Those of us on the beach now faced a daunting task. Impossibly large piles of food, camping equipment and clothing were scattered up and down the beach — much more than could fit into the tiny cargo holds of the boats. After a lot of head scratching, the packing began. Clothes were stuffed into dry bags, which were kneeled on until the last breath of air was squished out of them. Food was shuffled and a couple of small tins of olives were pushed up into the pointy bow of the boat. A loaf of chocolate-cherry bread that just wouldn't fit anywhere was divided up and eaten on the spot.

The water bags were slipped into the cockpit, to rest between paddlers' legs. Finally, the ax was tucked in behind one of the seats. But there was no way the tents would fit, absolutely none. So out came the bungee cords and nylon rope, and a few minutes later, the tents were strapped to the rear deck. A sigh of relief was heard all around and the gang took to the water (until someone saw the folding shovel sitting on a rock, and tucked it into a cockpit). Riding low in the water, the boats were paddled to the first camping spot, where everything was unpacked and stacked in little piles up and down the beach. Tomorrow the 3-D jigsaw puzzle of packing the boats would begin again.

Fog might appear somewhat benign, but it's a real hazard to the paddler who doesn't keep a close eye on the compass and chart. Here a light fog dissipates near Lyell Island.

of private land remaining inside the borders of Gwaii Haanas National Park Reserve.

After our stop at Ninstints, we paddled up the eastern side of the islands, around Lyell Island and on to another village site, Tanu. Along the way, we couldn't help but appreciate the foresight of the people who fought to protect the islands from clearcut logging, and pushed for the creation of the park. Meeting people such as Captain Gold, and knowing the history of the Charlottes, adds a new dimension to kayaking in the area. There is no better way than in a paddle-powered boat to approach a site, spend time and reflect on how others before you have sat on this beach and gazed at the opposite shore. I remembered Captain Gold's words, and could almost feel the presence of the people who once walked these shores and paddled in these waters.

Left: A Pacific harbor seal lounges on the beach at Lyell Island. These remarkable swimmers can dive to depths of more than 100 metres (330 feet) and hold their breath for up to 28 minutes at a stretch. They usually feed during an incoming tide, and can be seen quite far up rivers as well as near the coastal shoreline.

Above: Many creeks are needed to drain away the ample rainfall on Moresby Island. The Queen Charlottes are well known for the large amount of rain they receive every year.

Haida Gwaii or Queen Charlottes?

The battle over what to call these islands has deep historical overtones as well as political implications. If you look on a map you will likely see the group of islands off the north coast of British Columbia labeled the "Queen Charlotte Islands." Older texts will talk of the islands' "discovery" by Europeans. But thousands of years before Queen Charlotte's name was affixed to the place, the people who lived there knew the group of islands as Haida Gwaii — "place of the Haida people." Today's Haida are waging a persistent and unyielding campaign to have the words "Queen Charlotte Islands" scrubbed from the map and replaced with Haida Gwaii. They also are fighting to have other place names replaced with their Haida names. Anthony Island, for instance, in the Haida language is Skung Gwaii, which translates as "Red Cod Island." They feel it is their due and they have a quiet confidence that one day they will prevail. In the meantime, a visitor can be forgiven for thinking that Skung Gwaii, Red Cod Island and Anthony Island are three separate places.

A splash of color and diversity of form are revealed in this collection of sea stars at Burnaby Narrows (Dolomite Narrows), a shallow channel separating South Moresby and Burnaby islands. Sea stars such as the large sunflower star (upper middle of photo) have up to 15,000 individual tube feet, all of which have to be coordinated to propel it along the bottom.

Left: Two kayakers head for camp on the east coast of Moresby Island.

Above: Sunrises, such as this one looking out over Hecate Strait near Kunghit Island, make it worth getting up early.

West Coast of Vancouver Island

Nootka Sound to the Broken Islands

Morning fog dissipates over Clayoquot Sound.

The sleep was still in our eyes as we nosed our small cluster of kayaks out of Ahous Bay on Vargas Island toward the rising sun. We had been up for over an hour, stumbling around with our flashlights to break camp in the dark. As a group we weren't exactly what you would call "morning people," but we were hoping to cash in on the rewards of an early start — calm seas, light winds and a spectacular sunrise. Sometimes you get one out of three, or two out of three, but this morning was paying off on all counts: the boats glided through flat calm water toward the mouth of the bay as the rising sun began to glow on the mountainous horizon. It couldn't possibly get any better. But then it did.

Until you've experienced it, there's nothing that adequately describes the effect of a 40-tonne (88,000-pound) mammal exhaling as it surfaces just behind your boat. Out of the whale's relatively narrow blowhole blasts an amount of air equal in size to a small car. It produces a resonance that travels

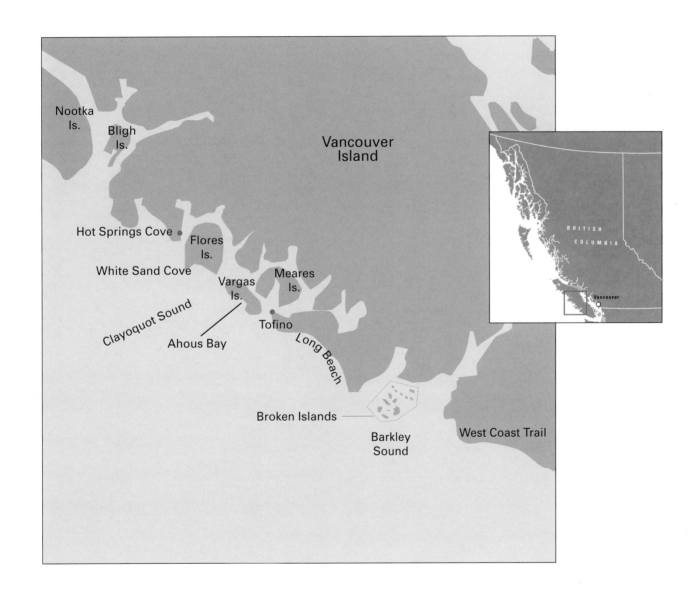

Nootka
Is.

Bligh
Is.

Vancouver
Island

Hot Springs Cove

Flores
Is.

White Sand Cove

Vargas
Is.

Meares
Is.

Clayoquot Sound

Ahous Bay

Tofino

Long Beach

Broken Islands

Barkley
Sound

West Coast Trail

BRITISH
COLUMBIA

Vancouver

Boats and gear wait while the crew stretch their legs and have lunch on the rocks at Bligh Island.

Paddlers soak up some sunshine in the shallows off the south-west coast of Bligh Island Provincial Park. The island was named after William Bligh, who served on Captain Cook's initial survey of the region. Later in his career, Bligh took command of the *Bounty*, whose crew later mutinied against him near Tahiti in 1789. Bligh was an exceptional seaman, bringing 18 loyal followers safely back to England in a seven-metre (23-foot) launch covering a distance of 6,600 kilometres (4,150 miles).

The rewards of berry picking: salmonberries, wild blueberries and huckleberries.

over and through the water and into the depths of your spine. A shot of adrenaline follows shortly there-after, varying in amount according to the proximity of the whale, as demonstrated in this extremely scientific formula: close encounter with whale = big adrenaline rush.

On this morning, the adrenaline was thundering through our veins as two gray whales surfaced unex-pectedly just aft of our boats. Our heads swiveled in unison to the source of the sound — in time to see their slick gray backs mottled with white markings and barnacles, and the mist from their exhalations hanging in the air. They disappeared for a short time, rose to the surface, and blew again before inhaling with a hollow whistling sound. They were now beside us — five metres (15 feet) off to the side, and prepar-ing to dive. We could easily see the markings that dis-tinguish each whale — barnacles, scars and white patches on their skin. They took a third and fourth breath and headed for the deep, arcing their backs before their tail flukes emerged, pointing skyward just a couple of paddle lengths from our boats.

Sitting in a small boat that could easily be upended by a flick of the tail, we were reminded of our vulnerability as we watched these giants glide by. After all, they've got a lot to get even for, considering they were hunted to the brink of extinction in these waters only a few decades ago. Whalers used to refer to the grays as "devil fish" because they would often turn on

The shallow draft and easy
maneuverability of the kayak
allows a close-up view of the
rocky shore near Nootka Island.

Gray Whales

An adult gray whale can be larger than a city bus, reaching up to 15 metres (50 feet) in length and weighing up to 30 tonnes (67,000 pounds). That's a lot of whale to see up close from a kayak.

They attain this immense size by eating an enormous number of very tiny creatures. It's estimated they consume 1,200 kilograms (2700 pounds) of shrimplike amphipods, tubeworms, mysids and herring eggs every day in northern waters. One of the ways they feed is by sucking in food-laden sediment from the ocean floor and pushing it out through baleen plates — a filtering material made out of the same substance as human fingernails (keratin). They feed mostly in northern waters, relying on their build-up of fat when in their southern breeding grounds.

These giants get around — they have the longest migration of any mammal, covering 12,000 kilometres (7,500 miles) between breeding lagoons in Baja, Mexico, and summer feeding areas in the Bering Sea, the Chukchi Sea, the western Beaufort Sea and the Arctic Ocean.

Because it's easier for them to feed in shallow water, they are often seen in lagoons and bays along the B.C. coast. They have an amazing spatial awareness and often come close to kayaks and other small boats without disturbing them.

The grays were hunted for thousands of years from small boats up and down the coast, but their numbers held steady until the early 20th century, when commercial whalers pushed them to the brink of extinction. Their numbers remain low in the western North Pacific and the North Atlantic population is extinct, but they have recovered strongly along this coastline, where their population is estimated at around 23,000.

A whale heads for the deep after surfacing close to a pair of kayakers in Ahous Bay, Vargas Island.

their attackers, smashing the small wooden whaling boats in a fury.

Before the commercial whalers arrived, the Nuu-chah-nulth and other west coast people had been hunting the grays and other species of whales for thousands of years. The whalers set out to sea in dugout canoes as the whales migrated in spring and fall — a time of year when the coast is often battered by large waves, howling winds and driving rain. If the hunters were lucky enough to spot a whale, the chase would be on, with paddlers pushing hard to keep up. In the bow a man with a hand-held harpoon would wait his chance to strike. If they got close enough to throw the harpoon, and its barbed point managed to stick, the battle was only just begun. The bone and wood harpoon would be secured by woven cedar ropes to a series of inflated sealskins, which would drag behind in the water, keeping the whale close to the surface and slowing it down as it tried to escape.

The end of the rope would then be attached to the canoe, pulled along on a "west coast sleigh ride" by the whale. After hours of fighting, their boat could capsize in a counter-attack by the whale, or the cedar ropes might be torn asunder. But if they were skillful and lucky, they would succeed in killing their quarry. If so, the now exhausted whalers had a new set of problems — 30 tonnes (67,000 pounds) of dead whale far from home, probably in darkness, and facing the worst time of year for sea conditions.

If these problems were surmounted, the whale would not be towed directly to the village, but to a nearby location suitable for processing the massive carcass. Blubber would be stripped and processed, some of the meat would be eaten fresh and some dried for the months ahead, and the bones not needed for tools or other uses would be left on the beach. Many of these whale-butchering sites can be found today on the west coast, including the aptly named "Whaler Island" in the middle of Clayoquot Sound, or the beach at Ahous Bay, where we found big chunks of whale bone.

You don't have to venture far on the west side of Vancouver Island to appreciate the seafaring ability of the aboriginal inhabitants. Much of the coastline here is wide open to the pounding of the Pacific Ocean and few people hazard a top-to-bottom trip down the coast by kayak. Fortunately there are a number of protected areas suitable for sea kayaking. The Broken Islands group in Barkley Sound, part of Pacific Rim National Park, is one of the most popular and easily accessible areas, with thousands of paddlers passing through these waters over the summer season. So many people visit that a number of restrictions, including a reservation system, have been established. The Broken Islands are particularly popular with novice paddlers because the cluster of more than three dozen islands allows them to avoid the large swells of open water most of the time.

Paddlers take an evening stroll along the edge of Ahous Bay,
Vargas Island, with the Catface mountain range in the background.

Clayoquot Sound, near Tofino, is another favored destination, with a formidable backdrop of towering mountains and a number of good beaches for camping. Starting at Tofino, we crossed to Flores Island in a light chop and landed on the broad shores of White Sand Cove. After a night on the beach, we made our way to Hot Springs Cove, in Maquinna Provincial Park, a popular spot where steaming spring water makes its way from a hot waterfall to the ocean in a series of cascading pools.

With our aching muscles renewed by the hot springs, followed by a good night's sleep, we paddled back to Meares Island and set up camp near some of the coast's most spectacular old-growth forests. It was a beautiful clear night and we put our sleeping bags out near the fire to look up at the blanket of stars, watching the occasional meteorite streak across the sky. The next morning we woke to find the area shrouded in a light fog. Walking the beach we soon spotted some wolf tracks. A pair of wolves — indicated by one large and a second smaller set of tracks — had been cruising the beach, probably hunting mice. Following the tracks back toward camp, we could see the wolves had picked up our scent and given our

A 16-legged kayak-carrying insect makes its way toward the water of Clayoquot Sound. These double kayaks can be heavy and awkward, so the more people helping out, the better.

camp a wide berth. But as we followed the tracks on the other side of camp we noticed they had circled back downwind of us while we slept. The closest print in the sand was a mere two metres (six feet) from one of our sleeping bags. We could only picture this "Far Side" wilderness moment, with the curious wolf sniffing the air and checking out these strange creatures cocooned in nylon bags on their beach. "Well, Dave, I'm not sure I want to eat something that snores that loud...."

Wolves are very leery of humans, so to have one come that close was unusual — but it wasn't surprising they managed to avoid our gaze. Camping on other beaches in more remote areas we had come across signs of wolves from time to time, but we only saw them on one occasion. Even that sighting was from quite a distance: a lone wolf loped along the driftwood logs at first light, far up the beach, pausing to look our way before heading into the protective shelter of the woods.

This was a relatively short trip on the island's west coast, but the rewards were huge. Whales, wolves and a hot springs bath were just a few of the memories of the journey. Looking down the beach as the sun burned away the morning mist, a hot cup of coffee in hand and pancakes cooking on the stove, we watched as the tide rose and began to sweep away the tracks that had caused such a stir only a few moments before.

Gulls and cormorants contemplate their next meal as they perch on the rocks of Cleveland Island.

Cooking a freshly caught salmon on cedar strips gives it a taste you can't get anywhere else.

Salmon

For the aboriginal inhabitants of the coast, the salmon was an integral part of life. Millions of fish were taken from the oceans and rivers as they returned to spawn, and considerable ceremony surrounds the fishery. Today, many native communities carry on the tradition of returning the bones of the first fish caught that year to the river from which it came.

Salmon was one of the first resources exploited by the Europeans; the Hudson's Bay Company shipped out 4,000 barrels of salted fish in 1835. The new technology of canning, introduced in the mid-19th century, created a gold rush mentality and canneries were established all along the coast to take advantage of what seemed like an infinite resource. At one point 90 canneries were operating on the B.C. coast alone.

But the resource did have limits. Overfishing, combined with other problems, such as destruction of spawning streams by logging and other industries, has pushed some salmon runs into extinction, while others teeter on the edge. However, there is cause for some optimism for the future of the fish, with a new emphasis on conservation and habitat restoration.

Storm clouds retreat into the distance as kayakers approach Burdwood Bay in Nootka Sound.

Paddling
Close to Home

Vancouver, the Gulf Islands and the San Juans

Vancouver's skyline offers a scenic backdrop for a twilight paddle.

You don't need to drive for hours or spend days paddling to a remote coastal beach to enjoy sea kayaking. Even in urban centers, such as Vancouver, Seattle and Victoria, worthwhile paddling is just as close as the nearest beach or dock. After a hard day at work, or on a Sunday afternoon, there's nothing better than tossing a boat into the water and going for a paddle close to home. You don't even have to own so much as a paddle, with kayak rental shops popping up along the water's edge in many places.

Meeting down at the docks early one July evening, we had a couple of boats off the roof racks and in the water in just a few minutes at Vancouver's Granville Island. Getting out of the harbor mouth was a bit hectic as 20 or 30 sailboats, power boats and water taxis jostled for passage under the Granville Street Bridge. But a few paddle strokes soon put the blue haze of engine exhaust behind us as we headed out into the broad expanse of English Bay.

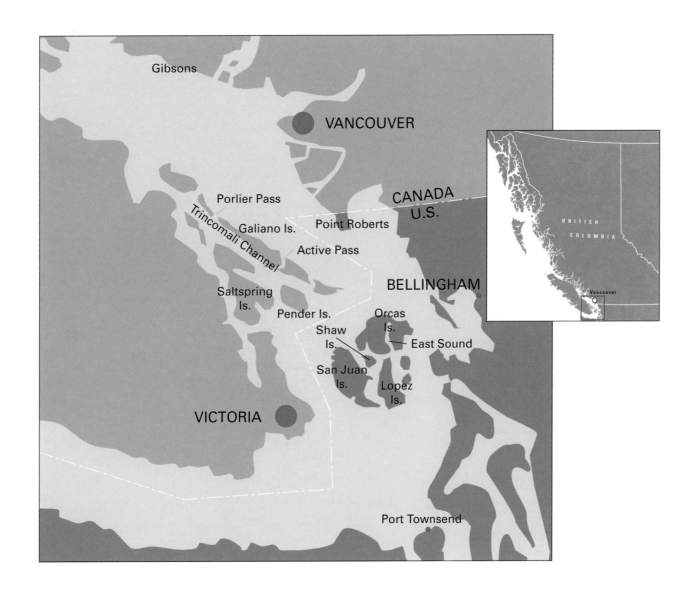

Gibsons

VANCOUVER

Porlier Pass

Trincomali Channel

CANADA
U.S.

Galiano Is.

Point Roberts

Active Pass

Saltspring
Is.

BELLINGHAM

Pender Is.

Orcas
Is.

Shaw
Is.

East Sound

San Juan
Is.

Lopez
Is.

VICTORIA

Port Townsend

BRITISH
COLUMBIA

Vancouver

Beaches such as this one on Valdes Island are scattered throughout the Gulf Islands. Unfortunately, most are on private property above the high tide line.

The noise of traffic, people and electronics faded to a murmur once we were a short distance off shore. These sounds were replaced with the slap of waves against the bow, and the steady rhythm of the paddles cutting into the water. It took us about 20 minutes to get out to the first of a dozen freighters riding at anchor in the harbor. Its sides were a freshly painted brown, and its superstructure a gleaming white. It sat waiting its turn to be loaded with wheat or sulphur at the docks before heading to some far-off port. From shore, the freighter didn't seem very big, dwarfed by the mountains behind it, but when we pulled up alongside, it proved to be a massive tower, riding an anchor chain with links thicker than our wrists.

Although we had paddled these waters many times, seeing this ship up close was a reminder of how travel on the water differs from travel on land. On the ocean, you can never go to the same place twice. The landmarks may remain, but the water will always be different. Fishing boats, birds, logs, tide level, barges, seaweed, currents and countless other things change with every trip. Finding a ship at anchor where none was before is like returning to an empty prairie to find a skyscraper has gone up overnight. And every city's waterfront offers something different, whether it's Victoria's scenic inner harbor with green lawns fronting the Parliament Buildings and Empress Hotel, or Seattle's skyline with 4,392-metre (14,410-foot) Mount Rainier towering in the background.

Drawing the Border Between the Gulf and San Juan Islands

Although they're in a different country, America's San Juan Islands are actually in the same chain as Canada's Gulf Islands. In the 19th century, settlers from both the United States and Great Britain set up farms in the area, and both countries laid claim to the islands. With some Americans calling for further expansion northward, tensions began to rise over which flag would fly. At one point war almost erupted after a hog belonging to the British Hudson's Bay Company was shot by an American settler. The dispute (dubbed "The Pig War") escalated and both sides brought in troops. However, full-scale hostilities were avoided, and a diplomatic solution was sought. Eventually, the two sides agreed to abide by third-party arbitration, and in 1872, the German kaiser decided in favor of the United States.

Bed and breakfast kayaking in the Gulf Islands provides views such as this one from Galiano Island.

The other advantage of urban paddling became apparent after our loop around the freighter stirred some hunger pangs. We paddled across to Sunset Beach near Stanley Park and hopped out of the boats as soon as they hit the sand. A quick stroll up the beach to the concession, and we were soon eating hot dogs, our spray skirts still hanging between our legs.

There are lots of opportunities for longer day trips and quick overnight trips on the coast as well. Sleeping in a tent on a remote beach isn't the only way to enjoy sea kayaking. A 50-minute trip on board a B.C. ferry will take you from the lower mainland to Galiano Island, one of the largest of the Gulf Islands between Vancouver Island and the south coast. The Gulf Islands are a chain of 200 islands and islets. The smallest are mere rocks fighting to stay above the tide, while the largest is Saltspring Island at 180 square kilometres (70 square miles).

One of the biggest chores when kayaking on long trips is unloading gear out of the boats and hauling the kayaks above the high tide line for the night. Unpacking can often take up an hour or more, and then there's setting up stoves, cooking, collecting water and all the other camp chores. But this little excursion was different, with just a small cooler bag and some picnic supplies the only addition to the paddles and safety gear. We hopped in the boats at Montague Harbour and cruised around a cluster of nearby islands, gliding by sandstone rocks carved into mellifluous shapes by eons of wind and sea action.

We took a leisurely four-hour loop, heading north in Trincomali Channel between Galiano and Saltspring islands. This is cabin country, and one of the interesting aspects is taking a water's eye view of the different styles of housing people have constructed over the years. There is everything from opulent vacation palaces sitting on big flat lots to more-endearing rustic cabins made from rough-hewn wood perched out on the edge of cliffs.

Galiano Island stands out among the Gulf Islands as a great training ground for novice kayakers, and we passed several small groups trying out the paddlers' realm for the first time. There are many short trips and hops you can take from site to site or from island to island, and most of them are protected by the mountains of Vancouver Island. This all adds up to a range of experiences for novice paddlers to tackle, while at the same time offering more challenging sites and conditions for experienced kayakers. Some areas, such as Active Pass to the south of Galiano, and Porlier Pass to the north, with their tricky tidal currents, are best left to experienced paddlers. Luckily for others, there are many places where wind and tidal conditions are calm most of the time.

One of the problems in the Gulf Islands is a shortage of public camping and park space accessible to paddlers, although most islands have at least one public campground. Depending on ability and sea conditions, it is possible to either paddle from one base camp to another or take the ferry connections between the islands. This time out we took the easy route, staying at bed and breakfasts on Galiano, Saltspring and Pender islands and doing day trips. There are dozens of bed and breakfasts dotting these islands, ranging from the simple to the elaborate, with a fair dose of the simply weird thrown in as well. After dinner in a local restaurant or pub, we were free to contemplate the day by sipping some wine as we sat in the hot tub or on the deck, taking in the view. Bed and breakfast paddling trips might seem a bit decadent, but they make fantastic weekend getaways. Even die-hard paddlers should make room for a "soft" trip once in a while — just so they can feel even tougher sleeping in a damp sleeping bag in a howling gale.

The San Juan Islands, a continuation of the Gulf Islands on the U.S. side of the border, offer a similar paddling experience. There are 172 islands in the group, but the four largest and best known are Orcas, San Juan, Lopez and Shaw. The coastline varies, with a mix of sandy beaches and rocky shoreline with a backdrop of evergreen forests and ochre-colored madrona trees. A one-hour ferry ride from mainland Washington took us to Orcas Island, a horseshoe-shaped island with rolling terrain dotted with small farms and country homes. Tourism is replacing farming and fishing as the lifeblood of these islands, and that can be seen in the large number of bed and

Sandstone cliffs tower above
a paddler near Galiano Island.

Kayak Craft

In the treeless Aleutian Islands, every scrap of driftwood that washed ashore was precious — there were no giant cedars to turn into ocean-going dugout canoes like the ones used farther down the coast. A couple of years of careful beachcombing were needed just to provide enough sticks to create a frame that could be bound together with animal sinew. The frame was then covered with sealskins, creating a light, fast and very versatile craft.

European explorers, who came in search of sea otter pelts in their top-heavy floating islands, otherwise known as sailing ships, soon saw the advantages of kayaks. These explorers noted how the Aleuts created a watertight seal between themselves and their craft by wrapping the boat's cockpit and their upper body in a piece of whale intestine. There was never a single fixed design for the Aleut boats — each was unique, based on who was building it and what it would be used for.

These hand-crafted boats were built by Randy Monge on Orcas Island. The frame at the right shows what's beneath the skin.

breakfasts, ice cream shops and small hotels catering to the weekend crowds.

On Orcas Island, we met up with Randy Monge, an experienced kayaking guide with a passion for boat building. We took a tour in the sheltered waters of East Sound, the fjordlike bay that almost cuts the island in half. Randy's hand-crafted boats proved to be amazingly stable, their wood frames flexing as they traveled through the waves. Kayakers are often heard to remark on how close to nature the boats allow you to get as you feel every ripple on the water, every variation in current as you glide in close to shore. These boats took the experience one step further, with their thin rubberized skins allowing us to feel the heads of bull kelp on our legs as we paddled along the rocky shore of Orcas Island.

The San Juan Islands offer a similar range of paddling to the Gulf Islands, although they are a bit more exposed to the weather. There are still plenty of sheltered places to test the waters, and if conditions are right, you can island hop quite easily. Camping can be found even on small, half-hectare (one-acre) islands, such as Posey Island. The big four islands offer hundreds of kilometres of paddling along their shoreline, but sadly face the same shortage of public beaches and campsites as the Gulf Islands.

Hours of paddling here could easily turn into weeks. It's much the same story with the other areas we have explored on the coast. For every place that we've visited there are dozens more where we would like to go. Every map or chart depicting our meandering coastline draws us in, leading us to ask what's down this stretch of coast, what can be found paddling into this estuary, up this inlet. And then there are the places that we have visited, the places we swore we would return to: bays with untouched beaches, abandoned villages with their ceremonial poles, the jagged cut of untouched rocky coastlines. All told, a true paddler's paradise, inviting us back and compelling us onward.

Index

For more information on kayaking in B.C., send a stamped, self-addressed envelope to:

British Columbia Marine Trail Association

1668 Duranleau

Granville Island

Vancouver, B.C.

V6H 3S4

The marine trail association is a non-profit group dedicated to preserving areas of the B.C. coast for the enjoyment of small boaters.